HOW
3D PRINTING
WILL IMPACT SOCIETY

by Cecilia Pinto McCarthy

ReferencePoint
Press®

San Diego, CA

TECHNOLOGY'S
IMPACT

ReferencePoint
Press®

© 2019 ReferencePoint Press, Inc.
Printed in the United States

For more information, contact:
ReferencePoint Press, Inc.
PO Box 27779
San Diego, CA 92198
www.ReferencePointPress.com

LIBRARY OF CONGRESS CATALOGING-IN-PUBLICATION DATA

Name: McCarthy, Cecilia Pinto, author.
Title: How 3D Printing Will Impact society / by Cecilia Pinto McCarthy.
Description: San Diego, CA : ReferencePoint Press, Inc., [2019] | Series:
   Technology's Impact | Includes bibliographical references and index. |
   Audience: Grades 9 to 12.
Identifiers: LCCN 2018011547 (print) | LCCN 2018013191 (ebook) | ISBN
   9781682825006 (ebook) | ISBN 9781682824993 (hardback)
Subjects: LCSH: Three-dimensional printing—Juvenile literature. |
   Manufacturing processes—Social aspects—Juvenile literature.
Classification: LCC TS171.95 (ebook) | LCC TS171.95 .M393 2019 (print) | DDC
   621.9/88—dc23
LC record available at https://lccn.loc.gov/2018011547

Contents

IMPORTANT EVENTS IN THE DEVELOPMENT OF
3D PRINTING TECHNOLOGY

1983
Engineer Charles Hull invents the first 3D printing method, called stereolithography (SLA). He later founds the company 3D Systems.

2005
Adrian Bowyer, a British engineer, mathematician, and professor, begins the RepRap project to make low-cost 3D printers by 3D printing.

1987
3D Systems releases its first commercial 3D printer, the SLA-1.

1999
Scientists 3D print a bladder using a patient's cells. A 3D printed scaffold is used to support the organs.

2008
A prosthetic leg is created using 3D printer technology.

1980   1990   1995   2000   2008

1986
Carl Deckard of the University of Texas develops selective laser sintering (SLS) 3D printing technology.

1991
Stratasys makes the first fused deposition modeling (FDM) machine. The 3D printing machine uses an extruder to deposit layers of plastic on a print bed.

2000
Z Corp makes the first multicolor 3D printer.

2014
The Portal 3D printer by a company called Made In Space prints the first 3D printed part in space aboard the International Space Station.

2017
Apis Cor, a startup company that 3D prints buildings, constructs its first house near Moscow, Russia. The one floor, 400-square-foot (122 sq m) house is built in just 24 hours.

2009
MakerBot Industries is founded by Bre Pettis, Zach Smith, and Adam Mayer in New York City. The company soon develops the first 3D printers for consumers.

2015
A complete jet engine is 3D printed by researchers at Monash University in Australia.

2009	2011	2014	2015	2017

2011
The first 3D printed car prototype, called Urbee, is printed by Kor Ecologic.

2013
Defense Distributed produces the first 3D printed gun.

2017
US aerospace manufacturer Rocket Lab successfully test launches its 3D printed Electron rocket from New Zealand. The Electron's engine took only 24 hours to print.

2012
LayerWise of Holland makes the first 3D printed jaw. It is implanted in a patient who lost part of her jaw to a bone infection.

3D Printing Technology Now and in the Future

Brody, a thirteen-year-old *Star Wars* fan, has a one-of-a-kind Stormtrooper hand. Born with a partial right hand, Brody was unable to hold a lacrosse stick or throw a ball. With his new hand, Brody can do those activities and more. Brody's hand was made by biomedical engineering students at the University of Cincinnati in Ohio. The students volunteer with a group called Enable UC, which makes inexpensive artificial hands using 3D printing technology. Using plastic materials, Enable UC students constructed a $20 hand and delivered it to Brody in just one week. Brody was the first person to receive a **prosthetic** hand from Enable UC. Since then, the organization has produced more than forty prosthetic hands and other assistive devices.

Typically, prosthetic limbs are made of titanium and carbon-fiber materials. Developing a well-fit prosthesis can be a long process. It can cost thousands of dollars. Expensive prostheses created by trained specialists are out of reach for many people, especially in developing countries. While 3D printed prostheses such as Brody's hand do not have all the advanced features of traditional prostheses, they offer an inexpensive, quick alternative. That was the goal of Jacob Knorr, the University of Cincinnati biomedical student who founded EnableUC. Says Knorr, "The idea is not to make something that's state of the art, it's to make something accessible that can help people."[1]

A REVOLUTIONARY TECHNOLOGY

3D printing is revolutionizing how things are made. In traditional 2D printing, information such as pictures or text is put into a computer. The printer uses **toner** or ink to print that information onto a sheet of paper. Unlike 2D printers, 3D printers create an actual three-dimensional object based on information put into a computer. An image of an object is created using special computer software. Then that information is fed to a 3D printer, which deposits raw material layer by layer to build an object.

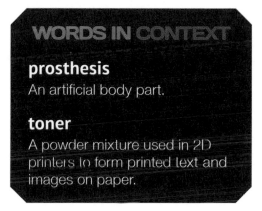

WORDS IN CONTEXT

prosthesis
An artificial body part.

toner
A powder mixture used in 2D printers to form printed text and images on paper.

3D printing technology is evolving quickly. Many experts believe that 3D printing will completely change manufacturing methods. But, as with any new technology, 3D printing could cause problems as well. Writers Hod Lipson and Melba Kurman are excited about the possibilities of 3D printing technology, but they warn about the technology's potential for misuse: "In a 3D printed future world, people will make what they need, when and where they need it. Yet, technologies are only as good as the people using them. People might fabricate weapons and create unregulated or even toxic new drugs. Our environment may be littered with quickly discarded print-on-demand plastic novelties."[2]

3D printers are already being used to inexpensively produce some medical devices. This includes dental fixtures.

HOW 3D PRINTING CAN BE USED

Society is already benefitting from 3D printing. The new technology is being used by the medical community to improve health care around the world. Lifelike models created with 3D printing allow surgeons to practice procedures before operating on patients. 3D printed bones and ears have been successfully implanted in patients. Digital dentistry performed with 3D printing means patients no longer wait weeks for dentures, mouth guards, and other fixtures. Instead, patients receive customized dental fixtures in days.

3D printing is also starting to be used to manufacture living human tissue, a process called bioprinting. Researchers are exploring ways to create human tissues and organs by 3D printing with living cells. This could help thousands of people waiting for life-saving organ transplants. At the same time, being able to print organs on demand will raise ethical issues, including questions about how bioprinted organs will be distributed and regulated.

In the fashion industry, 3D printing is helping designers create one-of-a-kind products. Designer Maria Alejandra Mora-Sanchez is eager to make 3D printed clothing. She believes, "3D printing is the future of fashion. With the current developments we are experiencing in this technology there are a great number of opportunities to create amazing new products and materials."[3] In the future, shoppers may buy custom-fit, 3D printed clothing adorned with personalized details.

The automotive and aerospace industries are beginning to rely on 3D printing technology to produce spare parts. Historically, making spare parts has been time-consuming and expensive. There are several steps required to create parts in factories, and then suppliers must store and ship parts. Many manufacturers discontinue production of parts that are in low demand. That means when a product breaks down, consumers may not be able to purchase the parts needed to fix it. But with 3D printing, manufacturers can simply make parts on demand.

3D printing technology is also saving time and money in the food industry. Hervé Malivert, director of culinary arts and technology at the International Culinary Center in New York, says, "With a 3D printer, you can print complicated chocolate sculptures and beautiful pieces for decoration on a wedding cake. Not everybody can do that—it takes years and years of experience, but a printer makes it easy."[4]

Plastic is one of the most common materials used in 3D printers. It can be used to build many different objects.

A GROWING INDUSTRY

In October 2017, John Kawola, an executive at the 3D printing company Ultimaker, said, "This is a watershed time for the industry. It feels like the tipping point, with lots of big companies and money involved. Big names are getting involved."[5] While 3D printing technology has the ability to quickly and cheaply produce objects, some experts believe 3D printing will also have negative repercussions in manufacturing. They wonder what will happen to people whose jobs rely on traditional manufacturing practices and retail.

3D printers are not just a tool for large manufacturers. Compact desktop models are within the budget of many consumers. 3D printers are becoming more common in homes, schools, and libraries. With their own 3D printers, consumers don't have to rely on manufacturers. Anyone with access to a 3D printer can design and print products on their own. People can also order 3D printed objects online. As more children become familiar with 3D printing technology, future generations will be able to further improve the technology. Lipson and Kurman, who wrote the book *Fabricated: The New World of 3D Printing*, say the future of 3D printing technology holds both benefits and challenges: "Like the magic wand of childhood fairy tales, 3D printing offers us the promise of control over the physical world. 3D printing gives regular people powerful new tools of design and production. People with modest bank accounts will acquire the same design and manufacturing power that was once the private reserve of professional designers and big manufacturing companies. In a 3D printed future world, people will make what they need, when and where they need it."[6] 3D printing technology has placed the world on the brink of a new industrial revolution.

How Does 3D Printing Work?

Before 3D printing can begin, a person must use modeling software to make a three-dimensional design on a computer. Additional software slices the design into super-thin layers. The instructions for the sliced design are then sent to a 3D printer. Instead of ink or toner, 3D printers use raw materials such as plastic or metal. The material is heated in the 3D printer until it is **molten**. Most 3D printers are fitted with nozzles or jets that deposit the molten material in a thin layer on a building platform. This layer forms one slice of the three-dimensional computer design. Once on the platform, the molten layer cools and hardens. The printer continues to add more layers of material, following the design created on the computer. It builds the object one slice at a time until the object is complete.

THE BEGINNING OF CAD AND 3D PRINTING

3D printing, also known as additive manufacturing or direct digital manufacturing, is not a new technology. In fact, manufacturers have been using 3D printing to produce parts for automobiles, airplanes, and other machines for about three decades. Corporations frequently use 3D printing to make **prototype** models for testing products before those products are manufactured in mass quantities.

3D printing technology would not be possible without computer-aided design (CAD). CAD is the use of computers and software to make two-dimensional and three-dimensional models.

Before CAD, designs were created using manual drafting. Drafting designs by hand was a time-consuming process. Engineers drew out detailed designs on paper. Correcting mistakes and making changes added time and cost to a project. In contrast, using CAD is faster and more flexible. Working on a computer means CAD designs are easy to modify if project materials or client preferences change. Also, CAD plans can be stored, altered, and used for different projects. Because they are computerized, CAD designs are quickly shared with others.

Without CAD, 3D printers would be worthless. As computer scientist and futurist Christopher Barnatt explains, "We would indeed not be at the start of a 3D Printing Revolution were it not at least in part for the efforts of those who have coded the computer aided design (CAD) applications required to construct 3D models, as well as the control and post-processing software required to communicate digital designs with 3D printers."[7]

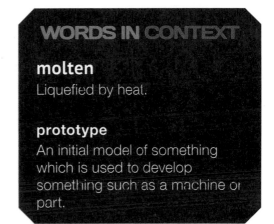

In 1963, computer scientist Ivan Sutherland created a CAD program called Sketchpad. Sketchpad allowed users to draw designs on a computer screen with a light pen. Computer users could manipulate designs and then store them on the computer's memory. With CAD programs such as Sketchpad, engineers crafted 2D technical designs. By the late 1960s, CAD systems had evolved so users could create computerized 3D models. Today's popular CAD software includes programs such as Blender, SketchUp,

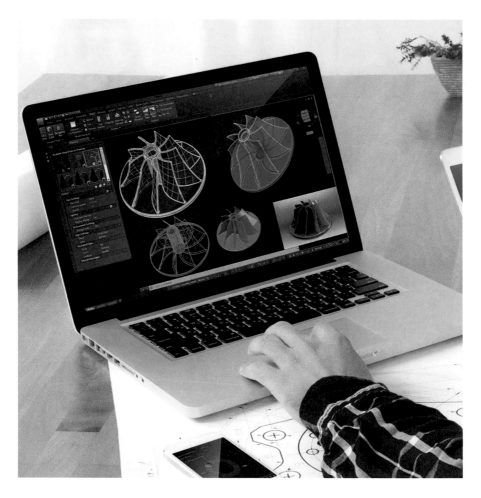

Before something can be 3D printed, it must be designed on a computer using a CAD program. Some designs created with CAD programs are shared online.

SolidWorks, and AutoCAD. The programs are used by both hobbyists and professionals.

THE FIRST 3D PRINTER

In 1983, American engineer Charles "Chuck" Hull invented the first 3D printer. Hull experimented with an ultraviolet laser beam and a tank of liquid photopolymer. Photopolymers are light-sensitive plastics.

They harden when exposed to light, such as the light from a laser beam. Hull's machine projected a laser beam from above, down onto a vat of photopolymer. The first 3D object Hull made was a small cup. The laser beam traced out a single layer of liquid photopolymer into the shape of the cup. The thin layer solidified. The solid layer was then covered by another layer of liquid photopolymer. The laser then traced out the shape of the cup again, creating a second solid layer. Hull repeated the process, building layer upon layer until the whole cup was printed. The process, known as stereolithography (SLA), is the most commonly used 3D printing technology that involves photopolymers. In 1986, Hull founded 3D Systems Corporation, now a leader in 3D printing. The company began selling its first commercial 3D printer, the SLA-1, in 1987. This 3D printer was used to construct detailed prototypes for industrial parts.

SUBTRACTIVE MANUFACTURING

Traditional mass manufacturing techniques are subtractive. They start with raw materials, such as metals, that must move through a series of steps. The raw materials may be milled, **machined**, and drilled. Some require folding and polishing.

During each step, some of the raw material is subtracted from the product until a finished product is formed. Traditional manufacturing also uses molds or dies to cut and shape materials. Molten metal or plastic is poured or injected into

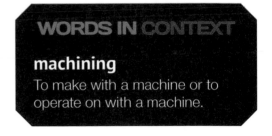

WORDS IN CONTEXT

machining
To make with a machine or to operate on with a machine.

molds to produce the desired object. After it is formed in the mold, the object must be trimmed and polished before it is ready for use. These traditional methods of making objects have been common for centuries, since the Industrial Revolution. Subtractive manufacturing methods leave behind metal scraps and other leftover bits of raw materials. Because of the many steps involved, traditional manufacturing processes are time consuming. It may take several weeks for final products to be ready for sale.

ADDITIVE MANUFACTURING

3D printing can be less time consuming and less wasteful than traditional manufacturing methods. Like subtractive manufacturing, 3D printing begins with raw materials such as metal or plastic. But instead of trimming away material during the assembly process, an object is formed by building up raw materials layer by layer. 3D printing is an additive manufacturing process because the product is fabricated by adding materials to form a whole.

Additive manufacturing is revolutionizing the production of goods. Technology experts Kalani Kirk Hausman and Richard Horne describe how additive manufacturing is more streamlined and efficient than traditional manufacturing:

> *Ideally the additive process will allow you to reimagine 3D printed products from the ground up, perhaps even allowing you to use complex open interior spaces that reduce materials and weight while retaining strength. And additive manufactured products are formed with all necessary holes, cavities, flat planes, and outer shells already in place, removing the need for many of the steps in traditional fabrication.*[8]

DESIGNING A MODEL

The 3D printing process begins with a computerized model of an object. The design may be created using a CAD software program, or it may originate from a scan of an actual object. For example, an orthodontist may use a scanning machine to take pictures of a patient's teeth. Once loaded into a computer, the data from the scanner is turned into a three-dimensional model of the object. This model can then be used to design a mouth guard precisely fitted to the patient.

Several websites allow users to download and upload 3D designs. The websites Thingiverse, GrabCAD, and Pinshape contain thousands of designs, ranging from toys and trinkets to tools and spare parts. Before the design can be sent to the printer, special slicing software divides the 3D model into individual layers. There are several types of slicing software, such as NetFabb, Repetier, Simplify3D, and Slic3r. After slicing, the design is ready to print.

The design is transferred to the 3D printer by a USB cable connection, an SD card, or Wi-Fi. Raw material for building the 3D object is fed into the 3D printer. Different kinds of printers are designed to handle different raw materials. While a chef may use chocolate to produce cake decorations, an artist may choose to create a 3D sculpture from plastic. 3D printers can handle raw materials ranging from plastic **polymers** and metal powders to ceramics, concrete, and even living cells.

WORDS IN CONTEXT

polymer
A large molecule made up of many smaller repeating units.

Some 3D printers are capable of combining materials to create a finished model. Frank Pertile, managing director of Australian company 3D Group, believes that developing more materials for 3D printing will fuel the industry's growth: "The materials side of things is a very, very important one in the grand scheme of things. . . . The materials are what will take 3D printing to a whole new level."[9] 3D Group is researching how to 3D print with graphene, a material valued for its light weight, electrical conductivity, strength, and insulating properties.

THE PRINTING PROCESS

3D printed objects are made either directly or indirectly. Direct 3D printing produces an object that can be handled. Direct printing allows scale models of an object to be quickly printed, a technique called rapid prototyping. Detailed rapid prototypes give designers the ability to test, modify, and refine parts before final products are manufactured. At the Ford Motor Company in Dearborn, Michigan, prototyping with 3D printers is an integral part of car research and development. Harold Sears, a technical expert in Ford's rapid manufacturing technologies division, states, "We touch a significant portion of the vehicle with 3D printing now. . . . We're prototyping virtually everything [using 3D printing] from road to roof."[10]

Indirect 3D printing combines both 3D printing and traditional manufacturing processes to create a final product. 3D printers are used to create molds out of plaster or resin. The molds can then be filled with material, such as molten metal, to create a final product. For example, OHLINA, a London-based jewelry design studio, uses 3D printed molds to create unique, sculptural jewelry pieces.

BUILDING LAYER BY LAYER

3D printers manufacture objects by building up super-thin layers of the raw material. Layers are typically 0.004 inches (0.1 mm) thick. There are three main ways that the layers may be bound together to form an object. When the raw material is a liquid polymer, the layers are fused together with a laser. When the raw material is in granular or powdered form, the particles can be bound by laser or a specific binding material, which can be like a liquid glue. Lastly, when the layers are made from melted materials, they automatically fuse together as they exit the printer nozzle and cool off.

The American Society for Testing and Materials (ASTM) classifies additive manufacturing processes into seven categories. The categories describe the methods that different 3D printers use to layer and fuse raw materials to produce a 3D object.

MATERIAL EXTRUSION

The first category is material extrusion. The way it works is similar to a hot glue gun. In a glue gun, a solid stick of plastic glue is pushed into the glue gun, where it is melted by a heating element. Pressing the trigger forces a string of molten glue to be squeezed out of the gun's nozzle. 3D material extrusion printers use a similar process. A solid **thermoplastic** such as acrylonitrile butadiene styrene (ABS) or polycarbonate (PC) is placed into the 3D printer. There, heat softens and melts the plastic. The molten material is then squeezed or **extruded** from the print nozzle.

The most common extrusion process for creating 3D objects is fused deposition modeling (FDM). This process was invented in 1988 by engineer S. Scott Crump, cofounder of Stratasys, Inc., a leader in 3D printing technology. A roller feeds plastic **filament** or metal wire from a spool into the printer. The material is heated until it softens enough to be extruded through the printer's nozzle onto a smooth surface called the build platform. As the material cools, it sticks to the platform and hardens. The printhead moves over the

WORDS IN CONTEXT

thermoplastic
A substance that becomes plastic when heated, hardens when cooled, and is able to repeat this process.

extrude
To squeeze or force out.

filament
A thin threadlike fiber or wire.

platform, depositing the next layer on top of the first. The process is repeated until the entire 3D object has been formed. Sometimes plastic supports are needed to prevent parts of the object from bending before the printing is done. Once the object is formed, the supports can be removed.

Some FDM 3D printers can be modified to extrude other materials, such as concrete, chocolate, or Laywood, a composite wood material. FDM produces many items, including airplane parts, helmets, pens, and cases for electronics. Lipson describes the versatility of FDM: "Any raw material that can be squeezed through a nozzle can be 3D printed. Frosting, cheese, and cookie dough are popular raw material. . . . Another emerging printing material is 'living ink' [a blend of living cells] that medical researchers use for bioprinting research."[11]

POWDER BED FUSION

The ASTM's second category is powder bed fusion. Powder bed fusion encompasses a number of techniques that use a laser or electron beam to melt powdered raw materials. Common materials include powdered metals, plastics, glass, and ceramics. A directed, high-energy beam **sinters** or fuses the particles, forming a solid. Selective laser sintering (SLS) was the first commercialized powder bed fusion method. SLS was invented in 1986. It was the brainchild of Carl Deckard, then a student at the University of Texas at Austin, and his professor Joseph Beaman. In a 2015 interview, Beaman described their goal: "To make the first one of something takes you six months, so why does it have to be all that slow? Essentially what we wanted to do was go right

20

CONTOUR CRAFTING

Behrokh Khoshnevis is an engineering professor at the University of Southern California and also the director of the Center for Rapid Automated Fabrication Technologies (CRAFT). He is credited with developing the 3D printing technology known as contour crafting. This 3D printing technology uses extrusion to construct full-size buildings using concrete. The specialized 3D printers are robotic and have a reach between 24 feet (7.3 m) and 40 feet (12.2 m). The printer moves over the construction site on a track system. The nozzle follows a computerized outline of the building's design. As it moves, it deposits a five-inch (13 cm) layer of concrete. About an hour is needed to allow the concrete to harden before another layer can be poured. An adhesive in the building mixture binds the particles of concrete together. According to Khoshnevis, the technology can build a single home or several houses, each with a different design, in a single run. Doka Group, an Austrian concrete formwork company, has invested in Khoshnevis' Contour Crafting Corporation. A spokesperson for Doka, Maria Tagwerker-Sturm, says Doka is especially drawn to the 3D printing method because of its speed and safety. "People can move into a new house only two to five days after the beginning of construction. This technology saves cost, time . . . and adds a lot of occupational safety as it is an automated process." Other applications for contour crafting technology include constructing homes for disaster relief and low-income housing. One exciting concept currently under exploration is using contour construction to build homes on the moon and Mars.

Quoted in Michael Petch, "Contour Crafting Begins Manufacture of 3D Printer for Construction," *3D Printing Industry*, June 2017. www.3dprintingindustry.com.

from a computer to the object by hitting 'hard copy.'" He added, "Selective Laser Sintering is . . . a way of making very complex objects very fast . . . now I could make things I had never made before."[12]

During SLS, a leveling roller spreads a thin layer of powdered plastic, ceramic, or glass across the printer's powder bed, a platform that holds the powdered material. Next, the beam of energy traces the first cross-section of the design onto the powder. Heat emitted from the beam bonds the powdered material to form a solid layer. After the first layer is finished, the powder bed is lowered. A powder cartridge deposits a fresh coat of powder, which is smoothed over by the roller. The beam traces out the second cross-section, sintering the particles and building a second layer on top of the first. The process is repeated until the complete object has been created. Any unused powder is recycled.

THE REPRAP PROJECT

RepRap stands for "replicating rapid prototyper." The RepRap project began in 2005. Adrian Bowyer, a British mathematician, engineer, and professor, acquired two 3D printing machines, each of which cost thousands of dollars. He then realized that he could use 3D printers to make less expensive copies of themselves. As Bowyer explains "[RepRap is] a 3D printer that can print out a significant portion of its own parts but not all of them. It's open source, so if you've got a RepRap printer, you just download the design off the web for free, and you can print another copy of it and give that to your friend." Bowyer wanted to ensure that anyone could build a RepRap printer. The parts that the RepRap cannot print are standard items such as electronic circuit boards and print heads that are easily purchased from a number of companies worldwide. The first RepRap design, named Darwin, was built in 2007 using a Stratasys FDM printer. The RepRap project has given individuals and small companies the opportunity to develop their own 3D printers. MakerBot, a well-known American desktop 3D printer company, began as a RepRap project. Design plans for the RepRap Ultimaker 3D printer can be downloaded for free. In May 2017, Bowyer received a 3D Printing Industry's Outstanding Contribution to 3D Printing award for RepRap and other contributions to the industry.

Quoted in Gal Sasson, "RepRap Project: Interview with Adrian Bowyer," *New York University ITP*, March 4, 2013. www.itp.nyu.edu.

SLS can be subdivided into two categories based on the type of energy beam used: direct metal laser sintering (DMLS) and electron beam melting (EBM). DMLS uses a high-powered laser to weld metal powders and alloys. EBM technology relies on the heat of an electron beam rather than a laser to sinter. During EBM, the object is built in a vacuum. This allows designers to use certain metals, such as titanium, which would otherwise react with the oxygen in an air-filled chamber. Both types of SLS are commonly used to make tools, parts for the aerospace industry, and architectural models.

VAT POLYMERIZATION

The third type of printing technique is vat polymerization. During this process, a tank of liquid photopolymer resin is used. The resin is sensitive to light. As an ultraviolet (UV) light source passes over the surface of the resin, it cures, or hardens, the resin to form the final product. The curing process is called photopolymerization. There are three types of vat polymerization: stereolithography (SLA), digital light processing (DLP), and continuous liquid interface production (CLIP).

SLA is the oldest and most commonly used vat polymerization technology. It's the process that was developed by Hull in 1983. During modern SLA, a laser focuses on the surface of the resin. As the laser beam moves, it traces an image of the first layer onto the resin's surface. The UV light solidifies the tracing. A blade or sweeper filled with resin sweeps across the vat, depositing another coat of resin. As each new layer is traced, it fuses to the previous layer. The building platform lowers into the vat as each subsequent layer is formed. When the object is completed, the platform rises, lifting the finished product from the vat of resin. SLA printing has traditionally been used to make prototypes such as car door handles and parts that need to be tested and refined. Recently, SLA printing has been used in the medical industry. In 2015, researchers at the University College London School of Pharmacy and the company FabRx used SLA to create tablets loaded with medicine. In their study the researchers concluded that this could help with various pharmaceutical procedures in the future. The researchers wrote, "In the future, this technology could become a manufacturing technology for the elaboration of oral dosage forms, for industrial production, or even for personalized dose."[13]

While SLA uses a laser beam as the energy source, DLP relies on light from a digital projector to solidify liquid photopolymer. The projector is placed above a vat containing the liquid. Instead of tracing the outline of the image, the projector displays an image of the first layer of the object onto the polymer. The polymer hardens into that shape, creating a thin layer. An image of the next layer is flashed onto the polymer, and a second layer is created. The steps are repeated until the whole object is complete. DLP is faster than SLA because it projects a whole layer at time. However, objects printed with DLP are not as finely detailed as those printed using SLA.

One of the newest types of vat polymerization is the ultrafast CLIP process. A sequence of UV light images of the object is projected through a special window onto the resin in a continuous sequence, just like a movie is projected onto a screen. Located below the resin tank, the window allows both the UV light and oxygen to pass through. Oxygen stops the resin from solidifying. So, by controlling both the UV light and oxygen, a "dead zone" of liquid resin is formed. As light passes through the dead zone, it cures resin to form the solid object. Rather than growing layer by layer as in typical SLA, a CLIP 3D object forms in a continuous fashion above the zone. Eliminating the step-by-step layering processes means that objects can be created quickly with CLIP.

Most 3D printing techniques build objects in thin layers. The object is made on the printer's build platform, which can often move around.

JETTING

The fourth and fifth printing techniques used to form 3D models are closely related. They are material jetting and binder jetting. As in vat polymerization processes, material jetting turns liquid photopolymers into solid objects using UV light. The difference is that during material jetting, the liquid photopolymer is not in a vat. Instead, the liquid is discharged in droplets from a nozzle on the printer. As the nozzle moves left and right, the drops are deposited on a build platform. Each layer is hardened using UV light emitted from an overhead lamp.

Several 3D printing techniques are used to create models or prototypes. This includes architectural models and prototypes of various products.

The platform is lowered as each layer is added. 3D objects produced through material jetting have smooth surfaces.

Unlike material jetting and other 3D printing processes, binder jetting does not use heat to fuse raw material. The printer includes an area that holds powdered material. A roller or blade spreads the powder over a platform. Nozzles drop or spray liquid binder onto the powder. Each layer is built up by adding alternating layers of powder and binder, until the object is complete. A binder jetting printer can use a variety of powdered raw materials, including metals, ceramics, and glass. Colored ink is sometimes added to the binding agent to create colorful models. Objects made using the binder jetting process usually undergo additional steps to strengthen them. They may be heated in a curing oven or fired in a kiln to remove any remaining moisture and harden. Infiltration is also commonly used to strengthen binder jetted parts. During this process, the printed part is heated in a furnace to burn out the binder. This leaves holes that are then filled with metal, usually bronze.

In 2017, 3D printing technology companies 3D Systems and Stratasys partnered with Royal Philips, a health technology company, to 3D print medical models. Doctors use special software and a material jetting process called PolyJet to create models of patients' organs such as livers and kidneys. These models help improve doctors' understanding of the health issues that patients face. Yair Briman, business leader of health care informatics at Royal Philips, describes how 3D printing technology is improving health care: "Enhancing how we visualize anatomy and diseases, like cancerous tumors, can profoundly affect the level of personalized care we can deliver to patients. By improving 3D printing capabilities . . . we aim to empower providers to improve care for complex cases and increase diagnostic confidence."[14]

LAMINATED OBJECT MANUFACTURING

The ASTM's sixth printing technique is laminated object manufacturing (LOM). This process welds or glues thin sheets of metal, paper, or plastic together to create an object. When working with plastic or paper, the sheets are usually pre-coated with adhesive. Some printers also spray colored ink on the paper to produce colored objects. A roller system moves the sheet over a build platform, where a laser cuts out the outline of the object. The platform containing the cut-out is lowered and a new sheet of material is moved above it and cut in the same manner. Layer upon layer is built up until the object is completed. Plastic and paper sheets are laminated using a heated roller to melt the adhesive and press the cut sheets together. If metal is used as the raw material, a different method called ultrasonic welding is used to join the layers. High-frequency sound waves are applied to the metal cutouts as they are held together under pressure. This welds the layers together.

DIRECTED ENERGY DEPOSITION

The seventh and final major 3D printing technique is directed energy deposition (DED). DED printer nozzles deposit metal powder or wire onto a surface. Cobalt, chrome, or titanium metal are the most popular powders. The powder is melted with heat from a laser beam or a plasma arc created by an electrical discharge. As with many other 3D printing technologies, the heat turns the powder into a solid. The printer nozzle is mounted on a robotic arm, making it capable of moving in many different directions. Layer after layer of powder is deposited, then solidified, to create a 3D model. DED printing creates highly accurate objects.

The world of 3D printing technology is moving at a rapid pace and in many different directions. Each of the seven major printing methods has its own strengths and weaknesses, and each is useful in some way. 3D printing technology is no longer confined to rapid prototyping and mass production. Software, printers, and materials are becoming increasingly available, affordable, and accessible. The 3D printing industry is moving toward personalization and customization. Experts believe 3D printing is still in its infancy and will have a positive influence on the future.

TYPES OF 3D PRINTING

3D Printing Method	How it works	Materials it can use	What it can make
material extrusion	squeezes melted material through a nozzle into layers that form an object	plastic, concrete, chocolate, living cells, composite wood	airplane parts, helmets, pens, buildings, food, bioprinted body parts
powder bed fusion	directs a high-energy laser or electron beam to sinter powder together to make layers	powdered metals, plastics, glass, ceramics	tools, architectural models
vat polymerization	an ultraviolet light passes over a vat of liquid photopolymer to shape an object in layers	photopolymer resin	models or prototypes, such as prototypes of car parts
material jetting	squeezes liquid photopolymer through a nozzle in layers that are solidified by ultraviolet light	photopolymer resin	models or prototypes
binder jetting	alternates layers of powdered material and liquid binding material to form an object	powdered metals, ceramics, glass; sometimes ink is added for color	prototypes, medical models, bioprinted organs
laminated object manufacturing	welds or glues thin sheets of material together to build an object	metal, paper, plastic; sometimes ink is added for color	models or prototypes, cell phone cases
directed energy deposition	powdered metal is deposited into layers that are heated and solidified	cobalt, chrome, titanium	models or prototypes

What Are the Positive Impacts of 3D Printing?

Traditional subtractive manufacturing has been used for centuries. Some might ask, why bother with 3D printing? While traditional manufacturing is still the norm, 3D printing has many advantages, and the technology is becoming more widespread. 3D printing is changing the way many items are manufactured. Already, 3D printing is a popular method for creating parts in the automotive, aerospace, and electronics industries.

A MANUFACTURING REVOLUTION

Traditional manufacturers produce mass quantities of parts that are then put together to form a final product. These parts are often made in different cities or countries, then shipped to factories. Assembly lines of workers put together everything from calculators to cars. Mass production results in standardized, uniform products. While assembly line production is efficient, each step in the assembly process relies on the step before it. Making changes to a product may require changes that slow down the entire production process.

While traditional manufacturing practices still dominate, 3D printing technology is making progress in the way products are designed and manufactured. One of the first steps in the manufacturing process is the creation of an initial model called a prototype. These models give designers a chance to examine a product for flaws.

Customarily, two-dimensional computer **renderings** of objects are examined onscreen. But this process is not foolproof. Not all flaws are apparent on a computer image. With 3D printing, designers and their clients can manipulate and refine a 3D model before the next stage in manufacturing.

Most industries use prototyping to ensure the accuracy of their final product. Prototypes are also useful for demonstrating a product to investors. In the past, prototypes could take weeks to create and cost thousands of dollars. In contrast, 3D printed prototypes can be made inexpensively in just hours. Rapid prototyping allows designers and engineers to create models from a variety of raw materials. 3D printed prototypes are accurate representations of the intended product and can be tested for fit, form, and function. With these prototypes, products can move quickly from concept to production.

Some industries use patterns or molds to form plastic or metal into products. Molten plastic or metal is poured into a mold to form an object. This traditional manufacturing method has taken a new turn by incorporating 3D printing technology. Ultimaker, a 3D printer company with offices in the Netherlands and Cambridge, Massachusetts, produces printers that create molds and casts used to manufacture parts, tools, jewelry, and food. Siemens Rail Automation employs the company's Ultimaker 2 3D printer to create molds for stainless steel railway components. Stephen Baker, head of research and development at Siemens, describes how the Ultimaker printer has impacted Siemens's production of steel railway parts: "We go from a 3D CAD model, to a 3D printed component, to the final metallic

3D printing can build prototypes and models faster than traditional manufacturing. 3D printing also generally wastes less material.

component without having to go through the normal process of manufacturing. . . . This has enabled us to reduce our time from the model stage to the final component stage to about one to two weeks, compared to where this would normally take us anywhere between 12 and 16 weeks."[15] Cutting down on multistep manufacturing processes dramatically lowers production costs. Fewer machines, less energy, and fewer materials are used in 3D printing versus traditional manufacturing. 3D printing eliminates the need to produce individual parts, thereby saving the cost of warehouse storage and distribution.

A NEW WAVE OF JOBS

Eliminating traditional manufacturing processes will affect the types of jobs available in manufacturing. 3D printing technology expands job opportunities for software engineers, technicians, scientists, designers, marketers, and entrepreneurs. Wanted Analytics is a software company that collects data about hiring trends. It reported that between 2010 and 2014, the number of jobs that required additive manufacturing skills increased by 1,834 percent.

People skilled in 3D printing technology can find employment in several fields, including medicine, transportation, engineering, software design, and programming. Companies are looking for coders, programmers, and 3D modelers who can not only develop software but also operate 3D printing equipment. Technicians are needed to keep equipment running smoothly. There are growing opportunities for artists and designers in areas such as jewelry and fashion to use 3D printing to manufacture their products. More and more scientists and researchers are discovering new ways to use 3D printing to solve problems in fields ranging from health to housing. As the 3D printing industry continues to boom, so will the need for skilled employees working in every facet of 3D printing technology.

CREATIVITY AND CUSTOMIZATION

People can share and alter 3D printing designs in a process known as open sourcing or open design. The designs are easily shared over the Internet, and it's easy to print them. Traditional manufacturing processes limit freedom of design. Manufactured objects are restricted by the tools and molds that are used to make them.

In 2013, Nokia partnered with 3D printing company MakerBot to give consumers the opportunity to make their own cell phone cases. Joseph Grima, former editor-in-chief of *Domus*, an architecture and design magazine, commented on the sharing of ideas through open design: "More and more design is resonating with the spirit of the social media era where it's much more about sharing ideas, collaborating, being completely transparent, completely open, rather than the secretive model of the past."[16] While most companies closely guard their product designs, some, like Nokia, see the creative possibilities of sharing information.

Open sourcing isn't limited to small items like cell phone cases. Local Motors of Arizona made history in 2015 by making the first-ever 3D printed car. The electric two-seat Strati travels at 40 miles per hour (64 km/h) and took 44 hours to print. The Strati was produced through open source collaboration—what Local Motors calls a co-community. Anyone, not just Local Motors employees, can be members of the co-community. The company hosts challenges and brainstorming sessions for people to offer ideas about Local Motors products. The Strati's design was chosen from more than two hundred ideas submitted online. Writer John Hayes describes Local Motors's strategy: "First, they crowd-source their designs by running design competitions and sharing royalties with the inventors. That gives them the capacity to work on multiple products at once and lets them tap into the enormous collective brain power of a community of engineers, suppliers, and customers worldwide."[17]

ON-DEMAND CUSTOMIZATION

Traditional manufacturing is limited to large, costly machines available exclusively for industrial use. But 3D printers have become increasingly accessible to the public. There are inexpensive, compact

People can easily access and share 3D printing designs online. Anyone with access to a 3D printer can print these designs on their own.

3D printers that can be easily set up on a home, school, or library desktop. Personal computers can run an array of CAD software programs for designing a variety of objects. *PC Magazine*'s list of the best 3D printers of 2018 featured home printers ranging from $198.95 to $3,495.

People can access online designs and 3D print objects at home. They often collaborate to improve an object's design. Thingiverse is an online 3D design community and one of the most widely used 3D printing websites. The website opened in 2008 and is owned by MakerBot Industries, a company that manufactures 3D printers.

On Thingiverse, people can create their own designs, or they can use someone else's design to print an object. They can also order print-on-demand items produced by companies such as MakerBot and Sculpteo. Anyone can create a design and upload it to the Sculpteo website. Authors Lipson and Kurman believe that this community of "makers" has great influence over new technologies in 3D printing: "Makers play a critical role in propelling 3D printing technologies into mainstream awareness. Makers, like other early adopters of disruptive technologies, demonstrate what may be someday possible on a larger scale."[18]

In addition to on-demand printing, 3D printing technology encourages product customization. Shopping at a store can be a time-consuming and frustrating experience. Customers must often choose from standardized goods with limited options. A jacket may be the right color, but it doesn't fit well. Once considered a futuristic idea, customized apparel and footwear is already here. Feetz is a San Diego, California, company that specializes in producing customized 3D printed footwear. Customers scan their feet using the Feetz smartphone app. A computer uses the scan as well as information about the customer's height, weight, and activities to create a personalized pair of shoes. The shoes are then shipped to the customer within a few days. Daniel Burrus, an expert in innovation and future technologies, believes that 3D printing of customized goods will become commonplace. He says, "3D printing is advancing quickly on a global level and offers something that up until recently was impossible: On-demand, anytime, anywhere, by-anyone manufacturing."[19] On-demand and customized 3D printing ends the need for manufacturing unnecessary products. Items made one at a time or in-store eliminate the added costs of manufacturing processes, storage, and delivery.

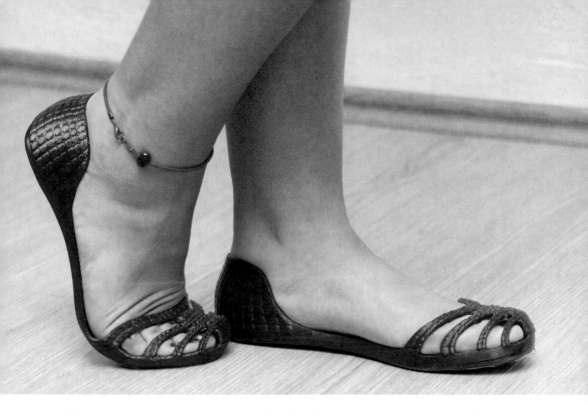

These shoes were made with a 3D printer. People can make all sorts of customized products with 3D printing.

COMPLEX CREATIONS

One of the greatest qualities of 3D printing technology is its ability to create objects with complex shapes that cannot be made using traditional manufacturing techniques. 3D printing provides a wider range of structural possibilities because it is not restricted by any molds or casts. The technology allows scientists to replicate intricate structures found in nature. Scientists have long recognized that some natural objects are resistant to cracks and fractures. These include bone, wood, and the inner layer of mollusks, which is called nacre or mother of pearl. It is the complex internal arrangements of these items that gives them their strength. By 3D printing a ceramic mixture, scientists replicate the intricate patterns. These bioinspired structures can be used to create strong lightweight products for the aerospace, medical, and automotive industries. British engineer Ezra Feilden believes 3D printing of bioinspired objects has great potential. He explains, "With many thousands of natural structures to choose from, there may be undiscovered opportunities to create materials with greatly improved mechanical properties using the techniques developed in this work."[20]

The ability to create objects with complex configurations is also appealing to craftspeople and artists. One of the most well-known 3D designers is Asher Nahmias, who goes by the name Dizingof. The Israeli artist specializes in "math art," transforming mathematical equations into 3D works of art. Writer Kerry Stevenson describes the artist's work: "Dizingof's creations are typically complex, flowing, and invariably beautiful. Browsing through his extensive portfolio of dozens of designs, you'll see vases, jewelry, bowls . . . but mostly it's just art, amazing mathematical art."[21]

ENVIRONMENTALLY FRIENDLY MANUFACTURING

The ability to generate complex designs with 3D printing also has a positive impact on the environment. A complicated part can be 3D printed fairly easily. Manufacturing the same complex part using traditional methods might not be feasible or might require several additional steps that add time and cost to a project. A team of engineers at CFM International, a company that makes jet engines for commercial airliners, was faced with this manufacturing dilemma. The team designed a new engine that significantly reduced airplane fuel consumption and emissions. The crucial component was a complex tip on the engine's fuel nozzle that sprayed fuel. The tip had an intricate internal form with more than twenty parts. "We tried to cast it eight times, and we failed every time," said engineer Mohammad Ehteshami.[22]

Several years later, the team was able to 3D print the complex nozzle as a single unit. As a bonus, the 3D printed nozzle weighed 25 percent less than the original nozzle and was much more durable. Ehteshami said, "The technology was incredible. In the design of jet engines, complexity used to be expensive. But additive [manufacturing] allows you to get sophisticated and reduces costs at the same time. This is an engineer's dream."[23] Both the aerospace and automotive industries are reducing their impact on the environment by using 3D printed components that are lightweight, strong, and require little or no additional finishing. Lightweight parts allow transportation vehicles to use less fuel, resulting in fewer harmful emissions.

In addition to cutting emissions, 3D printing is less wasteful than traditional manufacturing because it makes better use of raw materials and saves natural resources. Traditional manufacturing begins with a block or sheet of raw material, such as metal. Processing that material to make a product creates waste because the object must be cut away, leaving excess, unused material. However, the 3D printing process only uses the material that will make up the final product. Terry Wohlers, a 3D printing industry expert, acknowledges that not all 3D printing techniques are less wasteful than traditional manufacturing. But he believes 3D printing is much more **eco-friendly** overall:

WORDS IN CONTEXT

eco-friendly
Not harmful to nature.

> Some forms of additive manufacturing technology can produce considerable waste, such as the support material used in the process and laser sintering powder that cannot be reused. A much higher percentage of metal powder can be reused, so it is more environmentally friendly. When considering the design

of lightweight structures, especially for aircraft and eventually automobiles, the environmental benefit is greater with the savings in fuel, coupled with savings in using less material.[24]

3D printing allows products to be made locally. This saves natural resources such as gas and oil used to transport goods worldwide. Locally producing 3D printed items, especially spare parts, also reduces waste. A 2015 report by consulting firm Strategy& predicted that 3D printing technology will change the spare parts business:

SOLAR SINTER PROJECT

The world's deserts have an abundance of sand and sun. Sand contains silica. When silica is heated to its melting point and then cooled, it forms glass. In 2011, product designer Markus Kayser devised an environmentally friendly 3D printing process called solar sintering that uses sand as the material and the sun as the power source. His Solar Sinter 3D printer uses a printing process based on selective laser sintering (SLS). Kayser explained his motivation for using sun and sand: "In a world increasingly concerned with questions of energy production and raw material shortages, this project explores the potential of desert manufacturing, where energy and material occur in abundance." Kayser's solar sinter machine resembles a large metal box fitted with solar panels that capture the sun's energy. A huge lens attached to a moveable arm concentrates the sunlight into a powerful beam that averages 2,700°F (1,500°C). The beam is focused on a pan filled with sand. As the arm moves, the beam traces out the shape of the desired object, melting the sand as it moves along. As the layer cools, it becomes glass. Next, another layer of sand is sprinkled on top of the first layer. With each pass of the light beam, an additional layer of glass is added until the object is complete. The printer has light sensors that track the sun. As the sun moves across the sky, the printer turns toward it to ensure that the lens receives the strongest rays possible.

Quoted in Rose Etherington, "The Solar Sinter by Markus Kayser," *Dezeen*, June 2011. www.dezeen.com.

The business of making, storing, and shipping spare parts has long been a source of time-consuming and costly difficulties for suppliers of spare parts as well as for their customers. . . . [3D printing] will enable suppliers to make and send parts on an on-demand basis—and do so locally, close to where the parts are needed. Alternatively, companies can opt to print their own parts, bypassing the suppliers entirely.[25]

Online 3D printing service companies such as 3D Hubs want to replace mass production with 3D printing. 3D Hubs and other companies like it are increasing the public's access to 3D printing by offering local facilities equipped with 3D printers. They hope that their 3D printer networks will reduce pollution and the overproduction of goods that result from traditional manufacturing and distribution practices. 3D Hubs facilitates transactions between local 3D printing "Hubs" and people who order 3D printed products. Consumers can upload a design, choose a print location, then pick up their product at a location near them. 3D Hubs has a network of 7,231 local 3D printers around the globe.

MEDICAL BREAKTHROUGHS

3D printing technology has made significant contributions to health care. Approximately 100 US hospitals have a centralized 3D printing facility, and 3D printing labs are increasingly being incorporated into hospital settings. With 3D printing, doctors can create models of patients' body parts before surgeries. The models provide a clearer view of surgical challenges and help patients grasp the details of what will happen in the operating room. Orthopedic surgeon Dr. Boyd Goldie uses an Ultimaker 2+ 3D printer to create models of patients' bones before surgery. The replica helps both the patient and the doctor. Goldie can examine the model to better prepare himself to do the surgery. He also uses the model to help patients understand their medical issues and what will happen during surgery. "3D printing has utterly changed my workflow. As a surgeon, it helps me plan my operation and gives me a better understanding of what I'm dealing with so I don't have any surprises in the operating room. With modern radiology software, you can see a virtual model on-screen, but there's nothing like holding a model in your hands."[26] Recent developments in 3D printing have produced even better organ replicas. Most 3D printed body parts are made of plastic. But in 2017, researchers at the University of Minnesota reported a new development: soft organ models that look and feel like real organs. The organs have sensors that react to pressure, so doctors know how much force can be used during surgery to avoid damaging delicate tissue. 3D printed organs are becoming more widely used to train medical students.

3D printing is also producing inexpensive, customized medical devices. Hearing aids were once made using time-consuming and intensive manual labor. It was common for hearing aids to fit improperly and either fall out or cause irritation. Today, almost all hearing aid shells are 3D printed. There are also a few veterans' hospitals across the country using 3D printers to make custom devices including prostheses and orthotic devices. Orthotic devices, such as shoe inserts and leg braces, ease leg and foot pain, provide support, and help people walk. In 2017, the technology company Stratasys and the Veterans Affairs Center for Innovation established the first nationwide medical 3D printing network. The collaboration introduced 3D printers and technical support to additional veterans' hospitals. Hospital personnel will be able to share digital design files.

3D printers have also been used to replace some body parts. In early 2017, doctors in India replaced a woman's damaged vertebrae with a 3D printed titanium replica that precisely fit her spine. The

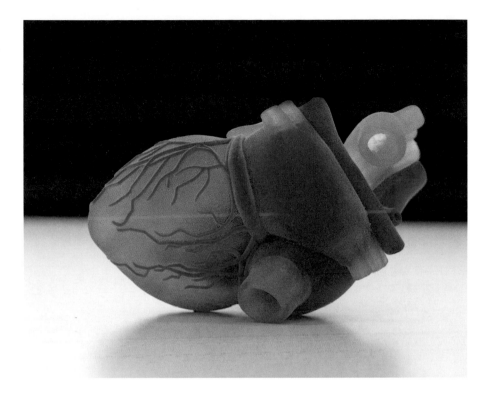

Doctors are beginning to work with 3D printed models of patients' body parts. These models can help doctors prepare for major surgeries.

customized replacement was made using scans of the woman's spine. The thirty-two-year-old patient suffered from spinal tuberculosis that had infected ten of her vertebrae. The disease destroyed her first, second, and third vertebrae, causing a gap between her skull and lower spine. Before the operation, the woman was unable to walk, had trouble speaking, and was in danger of dying. The surgery was successful, and the patient was walking and able to speak just twelve days later. "Given the complexity of this case, the use of 3D printing technology has helped us in bringing a successful outcome," said head surgeon Dr. V. Anand Naik. Around the world, patients have been successfully fitted with 3D printed titanium jaws, skull parts, shoulders, and knee joints.[27]

What Are the Negative Impacts of 3D Printing?

As 3D printing technology becomes more mainstream, it will have a noticeable effect on many aspects of everyday life. An increase in additive manufacturing alters the demand for traditional manufacturing practices. Economies worldwide are sure to change. The ability to print objects on demand diminishes the need for companies to produce large quantities of goods. It also makes it easier to produce illegal or counterfeit products. Open source design sharing brings to light questions about copyright, licensing, and intellectual property. 3D printing of biological tissues is surrounded by a myriad of ethical and legal issues. There are also questions about the environmental impact of 3D printing.

EMPLOYMENT AND ECONOMIC CHANGES

The production of goods using 3D printing technology has the potential to change employment demands. Traditional manufacturing practices still govern the way most items are produced. The steps used to manufacture everyday products require factories that employ millions of people worldwide. 3D printing technology reduces the need for these large production facilities. Assembly line workers can be replaced by a 3D printer. On-demand printing and customization of goods eliminates the need for large warehouses to store products.

Most products are made in factories by traditional manufacturing. Some people worry that people who work in those factories may lose their jobs as 3D printing technology continues to develop.

The ability to print needed products locally means extensive cargo transportation networks are no longer a necessary component of the manufacturing and distribution of goods. As 3D printing becomes a more widespread form of manufacturing, certain types of jobs in manufacturing, warehousing, and transportation may become obsolete.

The increasing availability of home 3D printers will also negatively affect retail businesses. Need a new pair of sneakers? There is no need to go shopping at a store when a custom-fit pair of shoes can be printed that same day at home. With decreased demand for their products, stores may be forced to close and let go of employees.

Even though 3D printing will also create employment opportunities, those jobs will require workers with special technology skills. People who are laid off from manufacturing and retail positions may not easily transition to a new career that requires these skills. Writer Brian Krassenstein believes this difference in skill sets may set the stage for broader social problems: "More than likely the jobs being lost will be for relatively unskilled labor, while any jobs being created by new technology will be for managing and skilled labor. This will create a further gap of income inequality in America."[28]

PRINTED WEAPONS

In May 2013, Defense Distributed, an open source company that designs firearms, released the design for the Liberator, the first gun that can be completely built with just a 3D printer. Defense Distributed's success in producing a 3D printed gun highlighted the real possibility that anyone can use 3D printers to create dangerous items or illegal weapons. Since then, several people have improved the gun's design and have successfully printed a variety of gun components. Designs for 3D printed weapons have become increasingly available.

While development of 3D printing technology has moved forward at a fast pace, regulations regarding its use have lagged far behind. In the United States, gun regulations vary by state. Most states have laws requiring a person to undergo a criminal background check before obtaining a gun permit. In some states, firearms must be registered. Store owners keep records of gun sales. However, guns that are 3D printed by individuals are not registered and cannot be tracked.

The Liberator brought to light the potential danger posed by the creation of 3D printed weapons. Online design files for weapons are available to anyone around the world with access to the Internet. Concerned about national security, the US Department of State ordered Defense Distributed to remove the files for making the Liberator from the Internet. The Undetectable Firearms Act of 1988 bans anyone in the United States from manufacturing, possessing, or transferring a firearm that cannot be detected by a metal detector. That includes 3D printed guns, which are commonly made from plastics. In 2015, the State Department disclosed changes to the International Trade in Arms Regulations (ITAR) which controls the import and export of defense materials such as weapons. The new regulations restrict the online posting of blueprints of 3D printed weapons.

DANGEROUS DRUGS

Medical drugs are manufactured in regulated, professional laboratories. In the future, 3D printing technology may allow people to make medications at home. In January 2018, chemist Lee Cronin and his team of researchers at the University of Glasgow in Scotland reportedly made 3D printed reactionware. These containers have reagents built into them. Reagents are substances that cause a chemical reaction to occur. Using customized reactionware and various chemicals, Cronin produced two different drugs: an anticoagulant and an ulcer drug. "This approach will allow the on-demand production of chemicals and drugs that are in short supply, hard to make at big facilities, and allow customization to tailor them to the application," says Cronin. While printing medicine on demand has many benefits, it may also allow people to create dangerous drugs and chemicals. Federal agencies such as the US Food and Drug Administration would be faced with creating new safety regulations for 3D printed medicines.

Quoted in Robert Service, "You Could Soon Be Manufacturing Your Own Drugs—Thanks to 3D Printing," *Science Magazine*, January 18, 2018. www.sciencemag.org.

While there is concern over increased 3D printing of weapons, security expert Gerald Walther believes that 3D printed weapons do not currently pose a large threat. He argues, "In general, at the moment, 3D printing does not create any novel security concerns. Weapons, including a huge portion of unlicensed ones, are quite abundant worldwide and pose a more problematic security challenge than any gun printed out of plastic. Current national and international legislation are also not circumvented by 3D printing, and there is no need to develop new international treaties just for printed guns."[29] He does acknowledge, however, that future threats from 3D printed weapons are real. People may create improved or unique guns and weapons. Also, advances in 3D printing materials will lead to stronger plastics and the use of metals. Walther states, "It may be possible in the future to print both the firing pin and bullets from plastic. . . . Advances in 3D printers themselves could have substantial impacts in determining the types of weapons and their quality that can be made by individual users at home."[30]

CONSUMER SAFETY

The 3D printing of firearms has proven to be difficult to monitor and regulate. The same is true for a variety of other products. The manufacturing of goods follows what is known as a supply chain. The supply chain consists of the designer who invents a product, the manufacturer who creates the product, and the retailer who sells the product to consumers. Products made through traditional manufacturing methods are subject to consumer safety laws. These laws and regulations have been established over the years to ensure that products are safe for consumers to use. Companies want to avoid the risk of liability. To avoid liability, they carry out quality and safety assessments and abide by federal regulations governing the production of their products. Manufactured goods can be traced back to the company that produced them. This tracking not only keeps products safe but also helps identify counterfeit products, which are generally low quality. When a product is defective, the company is held **liable** for any resulting loss or damage caused by the defective item.

WORDS IN CONTEXT

liable
Held legally responsible for.

Goods that are 3D printed at home, however, disrupt the supply chain. These products can be designed, manufactured, and sold by an individual. Individuals may also download designs made by other people. These designs may be altered before being used to 3D print a product. In another scenario, a store may sell 3D printed products, such as car parts. But who is liable if the part is faulty and causes an accident? Products printed on home or store printers do not undergo mandatory quality and safety inspections. Barnatt notes, "Even a simple item like a mug could prove dangerous if the handle came away when it was full of boiling beverage. 3D printing new parts to fix domestic appliances could also prove highly unsafe if they proved structurally unfit."[31] Would the designer, the manufacturer of the 3D printer, or the person who printed the product be held responsible? Also, who would be responsible for paying for damages? Questions of liability become even more complicated when CAD files are uploaded and used by people in different countries. Lawyers Maya Eckstein and Todd Brown say, "The non-traditional manufacturing and supply chain that is coming of age with 3D printing appears likely to make recovery difficult for consumers injured by 3D products."[32] They suggest that lawmakers may react by passing laws to give consumers a means to recover damages for injuries sustained from 3D printed products.

INTELLECTUAL PROPERTY

In 2013, designer Dizingof pulled all his design files off of the website Thingiverse. Stratasys, a leading 3D printing company, had printed one of his designs. They showed it as part of a display in their booth at a trade show. Dizingof's designs were protected under a license that prevents people from using his designs in a commercial manner without his permission or without acknowledging him as the designer. This wasn't the first time Dizingof had discovered other people trying to profit from his designs. He explained, "This issue began in mid-2012 when I started noticing individuals downloading my designs from Thingiverse—where they were offered for free, for personal use, and non-commercial use . . . and trying to monetize on them, be it on eBay or at street fairs."[33]

Stratasys's use of Dizingof's design highlights how intellectual property (IP) issues are becoming more prominent as 3D printing technology becomes more commonplace. Intellectual property refers to inventions, manuscripts, artistic works, designs, and other works that people create with their mind. Intellectual property has value and is protected by law. **Patents**, copyright, and trademarks are used to protect an individual's or organization's IP from unauthorized use by other people. Patented objects made with 3D printing technology are protected under current IP law. If someone prints a patented item at home, he or she is violating the law.

WORDS IN CONTEXT

patent
The exclusive right to create and sell a product.

As 3D printing technology develops, designs are being shared online more easily. Some people worry about protecting the rights to their own designs.

Problems arise when large numbers of people print patented goods at home. It is almost impossible to discover and prosecute those people who violate IP law. It is equally difficult to pursue IP lawsuits against corporations. To further complicate the issue of IP, the 3D printer company MakerBot introduced the MakerBot Digitizer 3D Scanner in 2013. With the scanner, users can scan any object, change the design if desired, and print out a 3D model using a 3D printer. The design can also be uploaded to websites like Thingiverse. As the capabilities of 3D printing expand, rules and regulations will need to be adjusted and created to keep up with IP issues that are sure to arise.

THE ETHICS OF BIOPRINTING

Increasing use of 3D printers in biomedical applications is creating a whole host of ethical concerns. Bioprinting uses living tissue as the raw material to 3D print human body parts. So far, scientists have successfully printed artificial skin, cartilage, and **tracheas**. Advancements have been made in creating bones, heart valves, and ear parts. The goal is to 3D print human organs. There is a severe shortage of organs available for transplant around the world. According to the US Department of Health and Human Services, twenty people die each day waiting for a transplant. There is no question that the ability to 3D print on-demand organs would save lives. But who will have access to these life-saving organs? The reality is that not everyone who needs an organ may be able to afford one. Science and technology experts from the University of Edinburgh in Scotland say, "Despite the promise of organs printed on demand for all, it is likely that the specter of a 'social stratification of biofabrication' will emerge, with those who can afford to pay for their 'own' organs benefitting."[34] The high cost of 3D printed organs would mean organs would only be available to wealthy people. This could lead to a possible scenario where those who can afford 3D printed organs will live longer. People who cannot pay for an organ will have to undergo traditional methods of treatment that include drugs and waiting for an organ donation from a living or deceased donor. This implies that wealthy people could pay to extend their lives with 3D printed organs. People with lower incomes would not have this luxury.

If common 3D printing of organs becomes a reality, how safe will it be to use these new tissues and organs? Currently, clinical trials carried out over long periods of time using large numbers of people are used to test the safety of new medical treatments. But because 3D printed organs and tissues would be created with a patient's own cells, it would be impossible to test organs, tissues, or treatments on large populations of people. New standards for safety and effectiveness would need to be developed before bioprinted materials could be used. Being able to print organs and tissues also raises the possibility that these technologies will be misused. There is the potential for 3D printed organs and other tissues to be fabricated without medical regulation. Counterfeit organs and tissue could be created and sold illegally. Experts also question whether 3D printing should be used to enhance the human body. As people age, their joints, tendons, and other body parts naturally decline. 3D printed organs and tissues could be used to replace aging body parts, allowing people to extend their lives. Perhaps one day athletes may be able to improve their performance with 3D printed organs or tissues that give them an edge over competitors. While these scenarios are not currently feasible, they represent many of the ethical challenges that may arise as 3D printing technology progresses.

ENVIRONMENTAL AND HEALTH HAZARDS

Most 3D printing techniques produce plastic products. Plastic is one of the biggest threats to the environment because it is not biodegradable. ABS is one of the most commonly used 3D printing plastics. It is made into filament, wound onto spools, and fed into printers. More and more people are gaining access to 3D printers and producing plastic objects. All over the world, landfills overflow with discarded plastic. Some plastic garbage also ends up in the water.

A glaring example of plastic pollution is the massive concentrations of garbage, including plastic particles, located in the north Pacific Ocean. Marine animals and birds die from ingesting plastic. Some plastic breaks down into tiny bits that enter the food chain when they are consumed by fish and other sea life. Chemicals from the plastic leach into the ocean. Authors Lipson and Kurman agree that 3D printing is adding to the problem of plastic pollution: "For better or for worse, our economy revolves around plastic goods. By giving regular people the power to make things from plastic at home, 3D printing opens up yet another new channel of plastic manufacturing. To become a greener form of manufacturing, 3D printing technologies need to embrace new, eco-friendly raw materials."[35]

Plastic litter isn't the only way that 3D printing may harm the environment and people's health. When ABS filament is heated in the 3D printing process, it gives off a noticeable odor. In 2013, researchers at the Illinois Institute of Technology showed that desktop 3D printers emitted high concentrations of ultrafine particles (UFPs) into the air. UFPs deposit in airways and lungs and can cause respiratory distress and damage, including conditions such as asthma. People should use 3D printers in well-ventilated areas or with an air filtration system. Items made with ABS plastic are not safe to use with food. ABS contains a chemical called bisphenol A (BPA). BPA can leach out of eating utensils, dishes, and cups that are 3D printed using ABS filament. The BPA is absorbed into the food or drink. The National Toxicology Program has some concern that BPA may be harmful to fetuses, infants, and children. Filaments made from BPA-free materials are being developed so people can print food-safe dinnerware at home.

Finally, 3D printers can be energy wasters. Some 3D printing methods use much more energy than traditional manufacturing practices. One study showed that 3D printers use 50 to 100 percent

Some people worry that 3D printers will create many plastic objects that will eventually be thrown away and cannot decompose naturally. This would have negative effects on the environment.

more electricity when making an item than injection molding does. A study by the Massachusetts Institute of Technology's Environmentally Benign Manufacturing program found that one type of 3D printing, laser direct metal deposition, used hundreds of times more electricity than would be used if the part were made through traditional methods such as casting or machining. Although 3D printing technology has many benefits, the negative effects are becoming evident. Lawmakers, industry leaders, and others must work to ensure that 3D printing is safe, ethical, and environmentally conscious.

What is the Future of 3D Printing?

For years, 3D printing was largely used for rapid prototyping. But 3D printing has become increasingly popular for manufacturing finished products and not just test models. In fact, 3D printing technology has spurred innovations in the aerospace industry, the automotive industry, and other fields. Authors Richard Horne and Kalani Kirk Hausman believe 3D printing technology is quickly altering society: "An amazing transformation is currently underway. [It] promises that the future can be a sustainable and personally customized environment. [This transformation] is not the slow change of progress from one generation of iPhone to the next. Instead, it's a true revolution."[36]

With 3D printing technology, businesses have cut production steps, expenses, and time. There have been advancements in digital design software, scanners, printers, new materials, and processes. 3D printing technology has expanded beyond the walls of industry and into homes, schools, and libraries. Previously, only large corporations could afford 3D printers. Now, desktop printers can be purchased for less than $250.

The future of 3D printing technology is promising. 3D printing is about more than printing simple things such as key chains. Developments in CAD software, printers, and printing materials are opening up a world of new shapes and customized, complex products. Researchers are developing new printing materials from

THE FUTURE OF FOOD

3D printers that use one type of material, such as chocolate or sugar, have been available for a few years. But new printers are being developed that can produce more sophisticated foods such as ravioli and burgers. One such printer is Foodini, manufactured by Natural Machines. Foodini can print both sweet and savory foods from fresh ingredients. Foodini comes with stainless steel capsules with different-sized nozzles. To make a food, the capsules are filled with prepared ingredients in a paste form. Foodini then deposits the ingredients on a work surface following a pattern. Once the food is printed, it is cooked in an oven or on the stove. To make pizza, Foodini first pushes out dough in a circular pattern. Next, it covers the dough with sauce from another capsule. Cheese and other toppings are added by hand, then the pizza is cooked in an oven. The machine comes with Foodini Creator computer software. The makers of Foodini hope the printer will encourage people to make healthy home-cooked meals using fresh ingredients. In the future, Natural Machines expects that consumers will be able to customize food mixtures to meet special dietary needs. Another company, BeeHex, created a prototype robotic 3D printer that was funded by NASA. Astronauts will use the printer, which makes pizzas, on space missions. The printer helps free up precious space that is taken up by packaged foods. Also, it gives astronauts other food choices besides freeze-dried packaged items. In the future, food 3D printers may help create sustainable food sources made from proteins such as algae and insects. They may also lessen world hunger.

combinations of raw materials. In the future, users may print objects with built-in electronic components, such as wiring and sensors. 3D printing will continue to revolutionize the fields of medicine, transportation, construction, and space exploration.

FUTURE 3D PRINTING IN MEDICINE

Replacing some human body parts with nonliving 3D printed implants has had many successes and continues to progress. But there is an even greater need for human tissues and organs to alleviate the universal shortage of organs available for transplant. Bioprinting could solve this challenge. The raw material used in bioprinting is bioink, a soft material that researchers load with living cells. Like other 3D printing processes, bioprinting begins with a design file that is sent to a specially constructed bioprinter that can handle bioink. Researchers first identify the structural elements of the body tissue they want to reproduce. The appropriate bioink is added to the bioprinter, which then sprays or extrudes the bioink layer by layer to create tissue. Culturing the tissue with nutrients promotes its growth. Bioprinted tissues help scientists understand how diseases and drugs affect the human body. Researchers can induce disease in 3D printed tissues and study disease progression. Drugs added to tissues in the lab provide valuable information on drug effectiveness and safety.

Even though bioprinted tissues such as skin, bone, and cartilage are being successfully grown in laboratories, bioprinting is still in its early stages. Adam Perriman, a chemist at the University of Bristol in the United Kingdom, notes that bioink research is critical to the advancement of bioprinting: "If you look at the technology of bioprinting, probably the limitation at the moment is the availability of bioinks."[37] The best bioinks print easily, maintain their shape, and help tissue cells grow. Researchers are developing liquid bioinks that gel quickly once they are printed. Another problem is that printed tissues do not live very long. To survive, tissue cells require nutrients and oxygen delivered by blood vessels not present in printed tissue. Also, 3D printers could not print tissues that were strong and large enough to grow and become integrated into the body. Several institutions have been successful in overcoming obstacles blocking the creation of viable bioprinted human tissues. In 2014, researchers at the Wyss Institute for Biologically Inspired Engineering at Harvard University

Scientists want to perfect bioprinting techniques, which would allow them to print living organs. Many hope that bioprinting could help people waiting for organ transplants.

developed a method for printing tissue made of many types of cells and blood vessels. Bioprinted tissues with those vascular networks are better able to integrate with a body's existing blood vessels. They also have a better chance of surviving. Jennifer Lewis, an author of the study says, "This is the foundational step toward creating 3D living tissue."[38]

Another breakthrough came in 2016 when researchers at the Wake Forest Institute for Regenerative Medicine came one step closer to making implantable 3D printed organs a reality. Dr. Anthony Atala and his team developed a new bioprinter and a water-based bioink combination. The Integrated Tissue and Organ Printing System (ITOP) deposits a temporary form made of a biodegradable plastic-like material that supports the tissue cells, holds them in place, and promotes their growth. The bioink has an arrangement of channels that allows oxygen and nutrients from the body to circulate and keeps the tissue alive while it develops blood vessels. Using the ITOP, the scientists successfully printed and implanted ear, bone, and muscle tissues in animals. A baby-sized human ear was implanted on a mouse where it grew for two months and developed new cartilage and blood vessels. While the new technologies hold promise, human organs such as hearts, kidneys, and livers are complex structures that are still challenging to replicate. The reality of printing and implanting fully functioning organs in humans is still decades away.

TRANSPORTATION

3D printing is transforming the future of the automotive, aerospace, and shipbuilding industries. Advancements in 3D printing of metals has been the catalyst for the increasing number of 3D printed parts being used in these industries. Titanium, nickel alloys, and steel are popular materials for parts because they are lightweight yet strong and durable. 3D printing allows companies to print complex shapes. It also costs less money and time to produce these parts with 3D printing than it does to use subtractive manufacturing methods like forging and machining.

For some time, vehicle owners have been able to 3D print replacement parts that are no longer in production. One of those people is Jay Leno, a comedian and former host of *The Tonight Show*. Leno maintains an extensive collection of more than two hundred vehicles. Leno enjoys restoring classic cars, but parts for these cars are often no longer available. Recreating the parts using traditional manufacturing methods is time-consuming and costly. Instead, Leno prints the parts he needs on a 3D printer. 3D printing has also come in handy for replacing parts of his hand-built EcoJet concept car. Leno says, "It is amazing how we just take 3D scans and come back with end-use parts that fit perfectly. With 3D printing, the automotive industry has changed more in the last decade than it previously did in the last century."[39]

In the future, people may be 3D printing whole cars, not just replacement parts. While a customer cannot yet walk into a dealership and print a customized car on demand, several companies around the world are using 3D printing to manufacture cars. The cars, with names such as "Blade" and "Light Cocoon," are in various stages of development, ranging from prototypes to actual working vehicles. 3D printing cars has many advantages over traditional manufacturing. It is faster to design and build a car using 3D printing technology. Because there is no need for a large factory, 3D printed cars are less costly to produce. The cars are also more environmentally friendly because they are manufactured from less material. The materials used are lightweight and durable. A lighter vehicle has better fuel efficiency. Kevin Czinger is the founder and CEO of Divergent 3D. Czinger's Blade car is constructed from seventy 3D-printed aluminum joints called nodes that are joined with carbon fiber tubing. The Blade's chassis weighs just 61 pounds (27.7 kg) and can be assembled in thirty minutes. The car can go from 0 to 60 miles per hour (96.6 km/h) in just 2.2 seconds. Czinger wanted to make a car that was not only eco-friendly but that was also produced

Some companies have made 3D printed cars, but the cars are not widely available yet. 3D printing of car parts is more common.

using environmentally friendly manufacturing processes. "The time has come for a new model of decentralized car production that fosters pioneering car designs and lowers costs while alleviating environmental damage," said Czinger.[40] The Blade produces one-third the emissions of an electric car. In 2017, the company partnered with a French car manufacturer, PSA Group, to use its 3D printed parts in the production of future cars.

The aerospace industry has also benefited from the rise in 3D printing technology. Because of the large size of airplanes, 3D printing is used primarily in the production of small, individual airplane parts. Aircraft fly more efficiently when they are made of lighter parts. Planes that weigh less also burn less fuel. 3D printed plane parts reduce overall weight and increase efficiency. They also allow for increased customization.

Like automobile and aerospace companies, shipping companies see the benefits of incorporating 3D printing technologies. One of the biggest challenges oceangoing vessels encounter is the need to replace parts or maintain supplies on long voyages out to sea. These ships often need to carry large numbers of spare parts and supplies when they will be away from shore. But sometimes a broken part may not be easily fixed or replaced. When ships are disabled due to a part failure, shipping companies lose time and money. The ship must remain at sea waiting for parts to be delivered by boat or helicopter. Dispatching additional vehicles to deliver parts also creates air and water pollution. Maritime industries are increasingly looking toward 3D printing technology to help resolve these issues.

A partnership of Danish companies called the Green Ship of the Future strives to lower maritime emissions by exploring and promoting new technologies that will make maritime transport more energy efficient. The group plans to place 3D printers and materials on ships. With 3D printers on board, there is no need to weigh down a ship by loading it with spare parts. When parts break, crew members can easily manufacture only what is needed. The 3D printers can also be used to print other supplies for the ship's crew as needed. 3D design files can be sent remotely from locations on shore. A lighter ship travels faster, reaches its destination quicker, and releases fewer emissions.

Military organizations, particularly navies, are exploring ways to use 3D printing. In 2014, the first 3D printer was installed on the US Navy ship USS *Essex*. The printer was there not just to print out parts and supplies but also to test how well 3D printers worked at sea. Coast Guard Commander Tyson Weinert emphasized some of the concerns about using printers on board a ship: "There are still several issues they need to overcome. They can't be subjected to the [movements of a ship]. . . . What is the tolerance for that, how will the printer itself react to those other forces?"[41] Weinert also noted that naval ships are already crammed with equipment and supplies. Finding space for a 3D printer is challenging.

The printer on board the USS *Essex* was initially used to print out spare parts for equipment as well as disposable medical supplies such as syringes. Within a year, however, the US Navy was using the technology to print **drones** at sea. Engineers on shore designed the drone then sent the design to crew members on board the Essex. The drone's parts were 3D printed on board, then assembled with electronics contained in a kit already on the ship. Drones can be sent on missions from a ship. A key component to building drones on ships is the ability to customize the drones to fit various types of missions. Drones may be fitted with cameras for search missions to combat piracy and drug smuggling.

WORDS IN CONTEXT

drone
A remote-controlled pilotless aircraft.

3D PRINTED HOMES

In the Russian town of Stupino, south of Moscow, construction company Apis Cor built a tiny one-story 409-square-foot (38 sq m) house. What makes the house special is that it was constructed in just one day by a robotic 3D printer. The home cost just $10,000 to build and was intended to demonstrate the capabilities of Apis Cor's new home construction printer. The 3D robotic printer is more mobile than the printers used to make buildings by 3D printing contour construction. Apis Cor's printer is compact and lightweight compared with typical construction equipment. It is 5 feet (1.5 m) wide and 16.4 feet (5 m) tall, weighing just 2.5 tons (2.3 metric tons). It is easily moved with a crane and can be transported from site to site on the back of a flatbed truck. The robotic arm sits on top of a cylindrical base, giving it the ability to turn in a full circle. At the end of the arm is a swiveling extruder head that prints on two planes at once. A concrete mixture is deposited layer by layer in a continuous process that builds both the internal and external walls at the same time. The printer's construction area extends to 630 square feet (192 sq m). As the arm rotates, the cylinder rises. The 3D printer's flexibility means it can print homes in any shape.

The robotic printer has many economic advantages. It is energy efficient, with low power consumption, and it operates quickly. It deposits only the building material needed, so there is no waste. By building an entire home by itself, the robotic printer saves on the cost of hiring construction workers. Once the home is built, workers are still needed to finish construction by installing windows, roofing, insulation, and painting. Engineer and entrepreneur Nikita Chen-yun-tai is the founder of Apis Cor. He says his company's goal is to make housing affordable for people around the world. Homes could be quickly and inexpensively constructed after natural disasters. 3D printed homes could also help alleviate homelessness around the world. When asked about his goals for Apis Cor, Chen-yun-tai says, "We are planning to print houses in Europe, Asia, Africa, Australia, North and South America. If necessary, even in Antarctica. We want to change the public opinion around the world that construction cannot be quick, environmentally friendly, low-cost, and reliable at the same time. And when mankind ceases to have enough space on Earth, we are ready to be pioneers at building houses on Mars."[42]

3D PRINTING IN SPACE

Far from Earth, 3D printing is having a major impact on space exploration. The website for California space-based manufacturing company Made In Space declares, "Dream on Earth, Build Among

This crew 3D printed a house from foam and concrete in just a few days in France in 2017. Some people believe 3D printing could eventually help to provide more affordable housing options.

the Stars."[43] In 2014, the first object was printed in space using a Made In Space 3D printer. Controllers on the ground sent commands to the printer onboard the International Space Station (ISS). National Aeronautics and Space Administration (NASA) astronaut Barry "Butch" Wilmore used the microwave-sized machine to print out a printer faceplate. "This is the first time we've ever used a 3D printer in space. . . . As we print more parts we'll be able to learn whether some of the effects we are seeing are caused by microgravity or just part of the normal fine-tuning process for printing," said the project's manager, Niki Werkheiser of NASA.[44]

In 2016, the Additive Manufacturing Facility (AMF) was permanently installed on the ISS. This 3D printer was built by Made In Space. Astronauts use the AMF to print out tools and other parts. Also, researchers and businesses on Earth can send commands to the AMF and print objects in space. AMF has crafted medical items, tools, parts, and a variety of devices. The 3D printer was designed to be easily upgraded to make it more functional. It uses a variety of plastic materials. So far, it has proven to be durable. Made In Space's business development engineer, Brad Kohlenberg, notes that there were a number of issues that were considered in the AMF's design: "The unique challenges of 3D printing in space include designing a printer that is sturdy enough to survive a rocket launch, reliable enough to work properly after that rocket launch, and safe and clean enough to use in the closed-loop environment of the ISS. With AMF, space developers on Earth now have a safer, faster, and cheaper way to get select hardware in space."[45]

NASA has bigger plans for using 3D printers in space. Apis Cor founder Chen-yun-tai's statement about building 3D printed homes on Mars is not such a far-fetched idea. In fact, NASA has been planning for future human habitation on other planets for years. In 2005, NASA began a program called the NASA Centennial Challenges. Each competition invites the public to develop innovations that can solve technical issues of interest to the space program. Individuals, student groups, and small businesses can participate in the contests. One of the challenges is the 3D Printed Habitat Challenge. The competition has asked inventors to use 3D printing to construct a sustainable and efficient home for astronauts in deep space, with a special focus on Mars. The shelter must protect astronauts from Mars's extreme conditions. NASA hopes that the challenge will nurture new technologies that are valuable not only in space but also on Earth.

The 3D Printed Habitat Challenge is divided into three phases. The first phase, which ended in September 2015, concentrated on architectural design. Participants were asked to imagine and create a habitat suitable for four astronauts to live on Mars, using only materials found on Mars. The winning team used information about conditions on Mars to design a home called the Mars Ice House. The team's design takes advantage of the presence of water and buried ice on Mars. The Ice House shields astronauts from dangerous cosmic rays and from the planet's extreme temperatures. Using the planet's water mixed with fiber and a special gel, a robotic 3D printer called iBo deposits layers of ice that freeze in Mars's frigid environment. Because ice is translucent, the habitat would be flooded with natural sunlight.

The second phase, which happened in 2017, focused on the development of building materials that could be used in a 3D printer. Each team built a space home made from materials naturally on Mars. They could also use recycled trash and waste products. Steve Jurczyk, associate administrator for NASA's Space Technology Mission Directorate, explained the goal of Phase Two: "Shelter is an obvious necessity as we prepare to explore worlds beyond our home planet, but space and weight aboard our vehicles are precious and taken by the many other resources we will need for survival. That's why we are seeking the technology to reuse the materials we will already be carrying and combine them with what is already available at our destination, which is, in this case, soil. We recycle here on Earth—why not on Mars?"[46] Phase Three, which opened in 2017, is the On-Site Habitat Challenge. Teams must use Building Information Modeling (BIM) software to design a 1,000 square-foot (93 sq m) habitat. They must also create a 3D printing system that can build a one-third scale model of the home. The structure needs to be made of materials found on Mars. It may also use recyclables.

Researchers are interested in using 3D printers in space because of the technology's efficiency. It's simple for astronauts to print out tools and other parts with a 3D printer on the International Space Station.

3D printing is heading in exciting directions. New printers, new materials, and innovative ways of applying 3D printing technology will surely shape the future. Along with all the positive contributions, there will be a host of issues that arise that will need to be acknowledged and resolved. Writing about 3D printing technology, Barnatt said, "The beginning of any revolution is always its most exciting period. The people who partake in a revolution's early stages are also likely to be those who will reap the greatest rewards, leave the strongest legacy, and have the most fun. The 3D Printing Revolution really is just about to happen. It is therefore high time for all those with vision to get involved."[47]

Source Notes

Introduction: 3D Printing Technology Now and in the Future

1. Quoted in 3Ders.org, "Student Group EnableUC Working on 3D Printed 'Luke Skywalker' Prosthetic Hand," January 19, 2017. http://www.3ders.org.

2. Hod Lipson and Melba Kurman, *Fabricated: The New World of 3D Printing.* Indianapolis, IN: John Wiley & Sons, 2013, p. 11.

3. Quoted in *Cosine News* (blog), "3D Printed Textiles," July 20, 2017. www.cosineadditive.com.

4. Quoted in Kyle Wiggers, "From Pixels to Plate, Food Has Become 3D Printing's Delicious New Frontier," *Digital Trends* (blog), April 19, 2017. www.digitaltrends.com.

5. Quoted in Andreas Rivera, "The State of 3D Printing in 2017," *Business News Daily*, October 23, 2017. www.businessnewsdaily.com.

6. Lipson and Kurman, *Fabricated: The New World of 3D Printing,* p. 11.

Chapter 1: How Does 3D Printing Work?

7. Christopher Barnatt, *3D Printing: The Next Industrial Revolution.* Lexington, KY: CreateSpace Independent Publishing Platform, 2016.

8. Richard Horne and Kalani Kirk Hausman, *3D Printing for Dummies.* Hoboken, NJ: John Wiley & Sons, 2017, p. 15.

9. Quoted in Leon Spencer, "Materials Set to Shape the Future of 3D Printing," *ZDNet* (blog), August 1, 2014. www.zdnet.com.

10. Quoted in Lucas Mearian, "3D Printing Is Now Entrenched at Ford," *CIO* (blog), August 21, 2017. www.cio.com.

11. Lipson and Kurman, *Fabricated: The New World of 3D Printing*, pp. 69–70.

12. University of Texas at Austin, "Joseph Beaman: 2015 UT Austin Inventor of the Year," *YouTube,* November 20, 2015. www.youtube.com.

13. Jie Wang, "Stereolithographic (SLA) 3D Printing of Oral Modified-Release Dosage Forms," *International Journal of Pharmaceutics*, April 30, 2016.

14. Quoted in Royal Philips, "Philips Teams with 3D Printing Industry Leaders 3D Systems and Stratasys," *PR Newswire,* November 27, 2017. www.prnewswire.com.

Chapter 2: What Are the Positive Impacts of 3D Printing?

15. Quoted in Kae Woei Lim, "Using Ultimaker 3D Printers for Manufacturing at Siemens," *Ultimaker* (blog), December 7, 2015. www.ultimaker.com.

16. Quoted in Emilie Chalcraft, "Nokia Is 'First Global Company to Embrace Open Design'," *Dezeen,* January 22, 2013. www.dezeen.com.

17. John Hayes, "Your Next Car Could Be Custom Made for As Little As $12K—and Be Recyclable," *Engineering.com* (blog), November 2, 2016. www.engineering.com.

18. Lipson and Kurman, *Fabricated: The New World of 3D Printing,* pp. 69–70.

19. Daniel Burrus, "3D Printed Shoes: A Step in the Right Direction," *Wired,* n.d. www.wired.com.

20. *Diamond,* "3D Printed Ceramics, Inspired by Nature," 2017. www.diamond.ac.uk.

21. Kerry Stevenson, "Noted 3D Designer Turns Paid Designs into Free Downloads," *Fabbaloo* (blog), September 25, 2017. www.fabbaloo.com.

22. Quoted in Tomas Kellner, "An Epiphany of Disruption: GE Additive Chief Explains How 3D Printing Will Upend Manufacturing," *GE Reports*, November 13, 2017. www.ge.com.

23. Quoted in Kellner, "An Epiphany of Disruption: GE Additive Chief Explains How 3D Printing Will Upend Manufacturing."

24. Quoted in Michael Molitch-Hou, "How Green Is 3D Printing?" *Engineering. com* (blog), September 28, 2016. www.engineering.com.

25. Reinhard Geissbauer, Jens Wunderlin, and Jorge Lehr, "The Future of Spare Parts Is 3D: A Look at the Challenges and Opportunities of 3D Printing," *Strategy&,* January 30, 2017. www.strategyand.pwc.com.

26. Quoted in *New Business,* "Instant Surgical Planning with Low-Cost 3D Printed Bone Models," November 20, 2017. www.newbusiness.co.uk.

27. Quoted in *Indo-Asian News Service,* "3D-Printed Vertebrae Helps Woman Walk Again," *NDTV,* February 16, 2017. www.ndtv.com.

Chapter 3: What Are the Negative Impacts of 3D Printing?

28. Brian Krassenstein, "3D Printing: Employment Boom or Employment Swoon," *3DPrint.com*, May 18, 2014. www.3dprint.com.

29. Gerald Walther, "Printing Insecurity? The Security Implications of 3D-Printing of Weapons," *Science and Engineering Ethics, US National Library of Medicine National Institutes of Health*, n.d. www.ncbi.nlm.nih.gov.

30. Walther, "Printing Insecurity? The Security Implications of 3D-Printing of Weapons."

31. Barnatt, *3D Printing: The Next Industrial Revolution*.

32. Maya M. Eckstein and A. Todd Brown, "3D Printing and Its Uncertain Products Liability Landscape," *IndustryWeek*, May 9, 2016. www.industryweek.com.

33. Quoted in Michael Molitch-Hou, "3D Printing Piracy Keeps Hitting 3DP Designers," *3D Printing Industry*, May 23, 2014. www.3dprintingindustry.com.

34. Niki Vermeulen and Gill Haddow, "3D Bioprint Me: A Socioethical View of Bioprinting Human Organs and Tissues," *BMJ Journals: Journal of Medical Ethics*, March 20, 2017. jme.bmj.com.

35. Lipson and Kurman, *Fabricated: The New World of 3D Printing*, p. 209.

Chapter 4: What is the Future of 3D Printing?

36. Horne and Hausman, *3D Printing for Dummies*, p. 7.

37. Quoted in Neil Savage, "The Promise of Printing," *Regenerative Medicine*, December 8, 2016. lewisgroup.seas.harvard.edu.

38. Quoted in *Wyss Institute*, "An Essential Step toward Printing Living Tissues," February 19, 2014. wyss.harvard.edu.

39. Quoted in Clare Scott, "Jay Leno's Garage Sees More 3D Printing, Repairing Handmade Car Thanks to 3DS' Geomagic Design X & Quickparts," *3DPrint.com*, December 8, 2015. www.3dprint.com.

40. Quoted in Kirsten Korosec, "This 3D Printing Startup Raised $23 Million to Disrupt How Cars Are Made," *Fortune*, January 25, 2017. www.fortune.com.

41. Quoted in Timothy Bengtson, "United States Navy Considers 3D Printers Aboard Ships," *3DPrint.com*, April 10, 2014. www.3dprint.com.

42. Quoted in Tatyana Petyhova, "Futures and Perspectives of 3D-Printing," *Apis Cor* (blog), n.d. www.apis-cor.com.

43. "Made in Space Mission," *Made in Space*, n.d. www.madeinspace.us.

44. Quoted in Bill Hubscher, "Open for Business: 3-D Printer Creates First Object in Space on International Space Station," *NASA*, November 25, 2015. www.nasa.gov.

45. Quoted in Luke Dormehl, "The International Space Station's New Low-Gravity 3D Printer Just Printed Its First Tool," *Digital Trends*, June 15, 2016. www.digitaltrends.com.

46. Quoted in Loura Hall, "NASA Offers Prize Money for Winning 3D-Printed Habitat Ideas," *NASA*, October 6, 2016. www.nasa.gov.

47. Barnatt, *3D Printing: The Next Industrial Revolution*.

Books

Chris Anderson, *Makers: The New Industrial Revolution*. New York: Crown Publishing, 2012.

Christopher Barnatt, *3D Printing: The Next Industrial Revolution*. Lexington, KY: CreateSpace Independent Publishing Platform, 2016.

Anna Kaziunas France, ed., *Make: 3D Printing*. Sebastopol, CA: Maker Media, 2013.

Hod Lipson and Melba Kurman, *Fabricated: The New World of 3D Printing*. Indianapolis, IN: Wiley, 2013.

Ben Redwood, Filemon Schoffer, and Brian Garret, *The 3D Printing Handbook: Technologies, Design and Applications*. Amsterdam, The Netherlands: 3D Hubs B.V., 2017.

Internet Sources

Ian Birrell, "3D-Printed Prosthetic Limbs: The Next Revolution in Medicine." *The Guardian*, February 19, 2017. www.theguardian.com.

Daniel Burrus, "3D Printed Shoes: A Step in the Right Direction." *Wired*, 2014. www.wired.com.

Maya M. Eckstein and A. Todd Brown, "3D Printing and Its Uncertain Products Liability Landscape," *IndustryWeek*, May 9, 2016. www.industryweek.com.

Eddie Krassenstein, "World's First 3D Printed Supercar Is Unveiled—0–60 in 2.2 Seconds, 700 HP Motor—Built from Unique Node System," *3DPrint.com*, June 24, 2015. www.3dprint.com.

Websites

3DPrint.com
www.3dprint.com

This website has the latest news about everything related to the 3D printing industry.

Apis Cor
www.apis-cor.com

Produced by the Apis Cor company, this website has news, interviews, photos, and videos that explain how Apis Cor's 3D building printer works.

Enabling the Future
www.enablingthefuture.org

The website provides information and stories about e-Nable and its network of volunteers who 3D print and assemble prosthetic limbs.

Mars Ice House
www.marsicehouse.com

This website's content explains the 3D printing technology and science behind the winning entry In the NASA 3D Printed Habitat Challenge. Video and slideshows show details about the Mars Ice House and explain scientific concepts.

Index

Index
Continued

Image Credits

Cecilia Pinto McCarthy has written several science and technology books for young readers. She also teaches environmental science classes at a nature sanctuary. She lives with her family north of Boston, Massachusetts.